CW01209810

To Alexander,

My Little Young Explorer

(c) 2020 Dr. Stuart P. Wynne
All rights Reserved

No part of this publication may be reproduced or transmitted in any form or by any means without permission of the author.

ISBN: 978-1-8382852-0-3 (print) 978-1-8382852-1-0 (Ebook)

Cataloguing in Publication Data

For more information on this title and others in The Young Explorers Series visit:

https://www.stuartwynne.co.uk/publications/young-explorers-series/

Wynne, Dr. Stuart P.

The Young Explorers Guide To Coral Reef Creatures

64 pages

The Young Explorers Guide To

Coral Reef Creatures

Book One Of The Young Explorers Series

What is a Coral Reef?

Coral reefs are found all over the world in places where the sea is warm and shallow. Although they look like rocks they are in fact made of thousands of tiny animals called polyps. They live together in colonies and build their homes out of hard minerals that they collect from the sea water. The homes that they build can be very large and provide other animals, such as crabs, lobsters and fish, with places to live as well. This means a thriving community of animals can all live together where, without coral polyps, there would be only sand and stones.

In The Picture: A huge Finger Coral reef in Anguilla, British West Indies. These large structures are important areas for baby fish and other coral reef creatures to live.

Fun Fact:

Known as the 'rainforests of the seas' coral reefs cover less that one percent (1%) of the ocean but are home to nearly 25% of all marine species. They are the largest structures built by animals on our planet. The biggest is The Great Barrier Reef in Australia that is so big it can be seen from outer space!

Words to look up:

Colonies
Polyps
Minerals
Community
Percent
Species

3

Coral Polyps

Our journey into the world of coral reefs begins by taking a closer look at the coral polyp. The polyps live in groups of closely fitting together individuals called a colony. They each build themselves a hard skeleton within which they live, that joins onto the neighboring polyps. Over time, as more polyps grow, the colony can become a very large structure, and when many other colonies grow all together in an area of ocean it becomes known as a coral reef. During the day the polyps hide inside their hard skeletons and keep safe from predators that want to eat them!

In The Picture: A close up picture of Elliptical Star Coral polyps with their tentacles retracted during the day, which means their hard skeleton is easy to see. At night they reach out their tentacles to feed.

Fun Fact:

Coral polyps need sunlight to grow. They have tiny little algae that live inside their skin that use sunlight to produce food that they share with the polyp. Without these little plants that photosynthesize using the sunlight, coral polyps are not able to grow and would eventually starve.

Words to look up:

Skeleton

Neighboring

Predator

Retracted

Algae

Photosynthesize

5

Coral Polyps at Night

At night the coral polyps open and let their tentacles wave around in the water. They feel safer at night because a lot of the fish and other creatures that prey on them are asleep. The polyps tentacles are sticky and catch food that is floating past in the ocean current. Plankton is their favourite food, which they sting and paralyse with their tentacles, making it a lot easier to eat. As you have already learnt, to survive the coral polyps need a lot of sunshine, which is why they live in shallow water in sunny parts of the world.

In The Picture: Great Star Coral polyps with their tentacles extended at night. Like most types of coral, during the day the polyps hide inside their hard skeleton for protection.

Fun Fact:

Coral polyps have transparent bodies, although the tiny algae that live inside them can be many different colours. This is why coral reefs look so colourful. Without these tiny algae coral polyps would be white, as all you'd see would be their skeleton showing through their skin!

Words to look up:

Tentacles

Prey

Ocean Current

Plankton

Paralyse

Transparent

7

Types of Coral

There are many different varieties of coral polyps, each of which grows into different looking coral colonies. Most of their names describe what these colonies look like which helps naturalists to talk to one another about them. The names of these different varieties include: brain coral, cactus coral, finger coral, lettuce coral, rose coral, star coral and lace coral. From these names can you guess what the coral colonies might look like?

In The Picture: Rough Cactus Coral is quite fleshy, and even with its tentacles retracted you can't see its hard skeleton. When it dies this hard skeleton is exposed and is extremely spiky and looks a bit like a cactus.

Fun Fact:

Corals have been alive on our planet for a very long time, first appearing over 500 million years ago. That makes them much older than even the dinosaurs! During this time they have evolved into thousands of different species that are found all over the world. It is this diversity that makes coral reefs so special.

Words to look up:

Varieties

Naturalists

Fleshy

Exposed

Evolved

Diversity

9

The Young Explorers Guide to Coral Reef Creatures

Solitary Coral Polyps

Some coral polyps do not live in colonies, instead choosing to live on their own. These solitary coral polyps can grow quite large and sometimes look a bit like sea anemones (page 18) when their tentacles are extended at night. Many people who enjoy diving or snorkeling under the water do not notice these polyps because they are much smaller than the surrounding coral colonies, or if they do they do not realise they are corals. Sometimes these solitary coral polyps are brightly coloured and very beautiful to look at.

In The Picture: A species of coral known as Solitary Disc Coral, which in this picture is growing on the side of a ship wreck in the Caribbean Sea.

Fun Fact:

Solitary coral polyps are the biggest known types of coral polyp. The largest, called a Meat Coral, has an internal skeleton that can be over 15 cm in diameter, but its meaty body can be twice as large as that and be over 30 cm in diameter! Meat corals live on coral reefs near Australia.

Words to look up:

Solitary
Diving
Snorkeling
Internal
Diameter

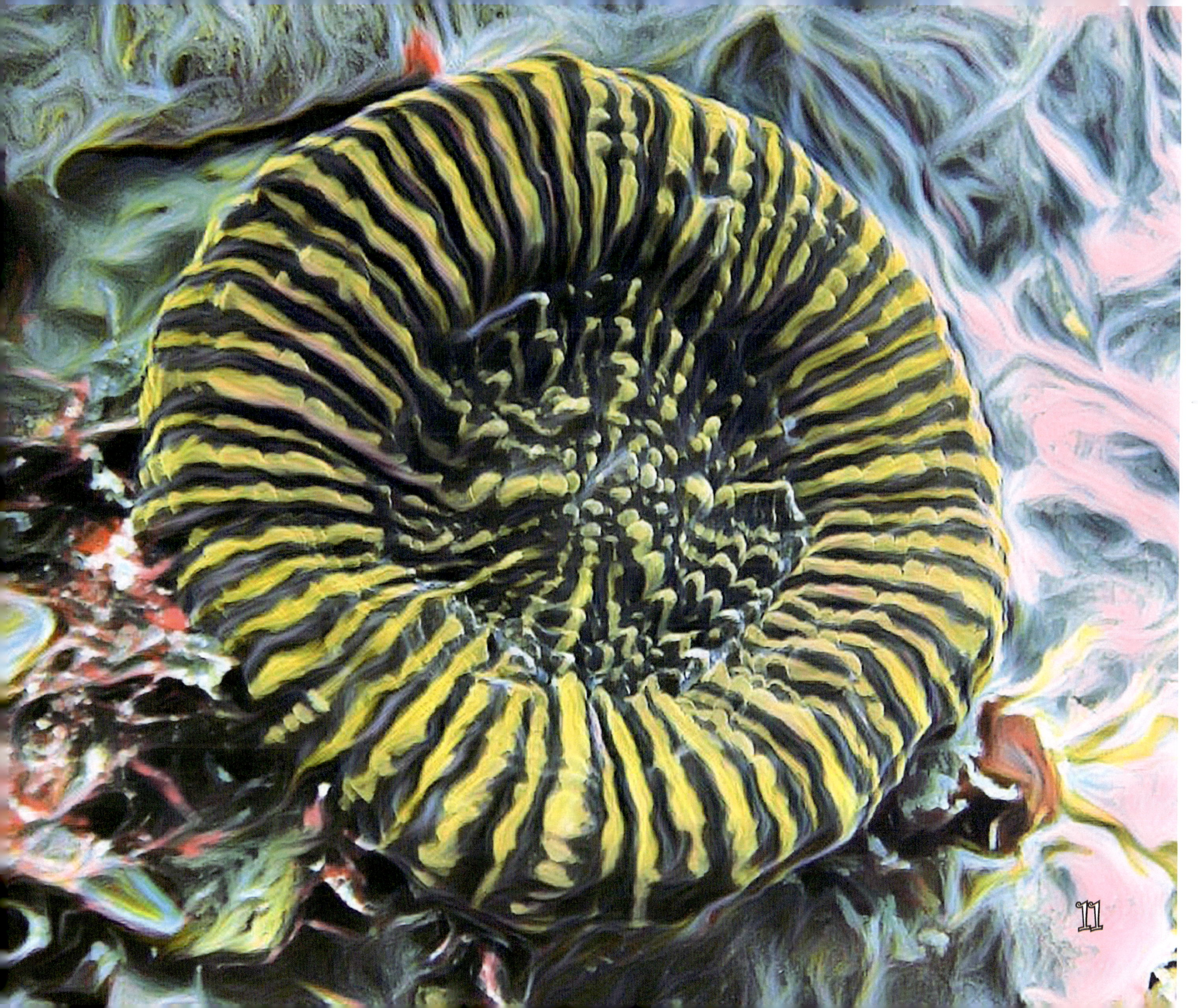

Flexible Corals

Some types of coral polyps grow into tall, thin colonies that look a little bit like plants. Their skeleton is made of a substance that is more flexible than other types of coral, which means they can sway in ocean currents in a very similar way to how plants sway in the wind. Like other corals they have tentacles that they use to catch food, and can also hide away inside their little homes if danger threatens. In some places the flexible corals grow in very large numbers and resemble huge forests, with fish swimming around their branches instead of birds.

In The Picture: A flexible coral known as a sea rod swaying in the water, surrounded by hard corals (page 14) on a coral reef in the Caribbean.

Fun Fact:

It is not surprising that many people think flexible corals (often called soft corals) are plants rather than animals. They look like they are rooted into the ground like a plant and they sway around in the water like them too! It wasn't until the eighteenth century that scientists finally realised that corals were in fact animals!

Words to look up:

Flexible
Substance
Threatens
Resemble
Rooted

13

Hard Corals

One of the most important types of coral for inhabitants of the coral reef are the hard corals. They grow in large colonies and have a hard skeleton that helps build the structure of the reef itself. Without them the coral reef would gradually erode away and disappear, leaving all the fish and other coral reef life without anywhere to live. These hard corals all start as small colonies and slowly grow over time, sometimes taking hundreds of years to reach full size. This means our actions today are very important for coral reefs to be able to survive on into the future.

In The Picture: Elkhorn Coral growing very close to the surface on what is known as an emergent reef. Many types of coral like to grow close to the surface as they get more sunlight which they need to survive.

Fun Fact:

Elkhorn Coral colonies can live for hundreds of years and are one of fastest growing coral species in the world! A healthy established colony can grow up to 13 cm a year, which is very quick indeed for a hard coral species as many grow less than 1 cm during the same period of time!

Words to look up:

Inhabitants
Structure
Gradually
Emergent
Established

15

The Young Explorers Guide to Coral Reef Creatures

Coral Cousins: Zoanthids

Some creatures that live on coral reefs look very similar to corals. One such example are the zoanthids, who grow in colonies and also have tentacles with which they catch food. The Zoanthids however do not have a hard skeleton house to hide in during the day like the corals, and so often chose to live in small holes among the rocks and coral colonies, in very shallow, protected parts of the reef. Like the corals, zoanthids have tentacles that they use to sting their prey which makes it easier to eat.

In The Picture:
A colony of Mat Zoanthids with their tentacles fully extended. Unlike their coral cousins, Mat Zoanthids do not always hide their tentacles during the day as they usually live in quite sheltered and shady places.

Fun Fact:

Although very beautiful to look at, some species of zoanthid contain one of the most toxic chemicals known to man. It is so dangerous that it can be fatal even if consumed in very small amounts! This means that people who keep zoanthids in an aquarium have to be very careful indeed!

Words to look up:

Protected

Sheltered

Toxic

Chemicals

Consumed

Aquarium

17

Coral Cousins: Sea Anemones

Another group of creatures that look a bit like corals are the sea anemones, which resemble very large solitary corals (page 10) with extra long tentacles. Like the zoanthids (previous page), the sea anemones do not have a hard skeleton to hide in from predators, and so they often live in hidey-holes within the coral reef structure. They extend their tentacles out from their hiding place to catch prey, but can retract them back into safety if danger threatens. Sea anemone tentacles can also sting, which is useful when trying to catch small fish, which is one of their favorite foods.

In The Picture: A Giant Anemone living happily on a coral reef in the Caribbean Sea. Its tentacles are fully extended while they wave around freely in the water looking for passing food.

Fun Fact:

Small fish often live in association with large anemones, using their stinging tentacles as protection. These fish are immune to the anemone sting and so can live there safe from predators. Indopacific Clown Fish, as in the movie Finding Nemo, are a famous example of this.

Words to look up:

Association

Immune

Indopacific

19

Coral Cousins: Corallimorphs

The corallimorphs are very similar to the sea anemones, except that they have much shorter tentacles. The tentacles are so short it is possible to see the animals mouth at its centre. The corallimorphs usually grow in groups together in shallow areas where they are safer from possible danger. Their tentacles can be very colourful, and look beautiful as they sway around slowly when the water moves past them. As with the anemones, the corallimorphs use these tentacles to capture passing food items which they then pass to their central mouth.

In The Picture: A Florida Corallimorph living nestled into the reef structure with its body folded over the rocky surface, and neighboring corallimorph friends on either side.

Fun Fact:

The corallimorphs often live in groups that cover large areas of shallow reef habitat. They may be so closely packed to one another that it is not very easy to distinguish one individual from another, instead looking like a huge blanket of short stubby tentacles covering the rocks.

Words to look up:

Capture
Nestled
Habitat

21

… The Young Explorers Guide to Coral Reef Creatures

Coral Cousins: Hydroids

Hydroids are another type of creature that look similar to corals, with stinging tentacles that they use to catch prey. However, they are usually very small in size and colonies do not produce a hard skeleton in which they live in the same way as corals do. Some species are very small so the individual animals are very hard to see, like the Christmas Tree Hydroid whose colony looks just like a Christmas tree! Others are much bigger and live alone and can grow to the size of a marble with very elegant twisted tentacles.

In The Picture: A large Solitary Gorgonian Hydroid that lives its life growing from the surface of certain types of flexible corals (page 12) known as Gorgonian Sea Fans.

Fun Fact:

Hydroids that live in colonies use a different type of material to support their bodies than corals. The material they use is called chitin, and is in fact the same substance that land insects use to build their exoskeletons!

Words to look up:

Elegant
Exoskeleton

23

Plants and Algae

Although many corals and coral cousins look like plants, you now know that they are in fact animals. However, there are a lot of plants and algae that also live on coral reefs and provide food and shelter for many underwater animals. Sometimes they grow in vast underwater meadows, such as the sea grass plant, that some species of sea turtle eat. Other kinds are tiny algae that live in crevices and grow in very intricate shapes and sizes. Can you tell which one is pictured opposite?

In The Picture: You guessed correctly if you thought that the picture is of a type of algae. It belongs to a group known as caulerpa, that grow in many different intricate patterns.

Fun Fact:

Sea grass is a type of flowering plant similar to those we see on land. Like those on land, its flowers need pollinating too, but there are no bees underwater to do this. Instead, tiny creatures related to shrimps (page 44) do the job, carrying pollen grains from one flower to another.

Words to look up:

Vast
Meadows
Sea Turtle
Crevices
Intricate
Pollinating

25

Sponges

Sponges are a very strange group of creatures that look more like plants than animals. They fix themselves to the reef structure and do not move, slowly growing over time and sometimes become very large indeed. They pump water through holes that are found all over their bodies and filter out anything that they can use as food. Some sponges can bore into rock and hide underneath its surface with only their holes protruding. Others have hydroids (page 22) growing out of their surface with which they share food. Can you see the hydroids living with the sponge in the picture?

In The Picture: A Pink Vase Sponge living a very quiet life with hundreds of Sponge Zoanthids clinging to its surface. All sponges of this species have zoanthid passengers.

Fun Fact:

Sponges are some of the simplest animals on our planet, with no head, eyes, mouth, legs, arms or tails. However, some scientists speculate that they have achieved evolutionary perfection as they have remained almost unchanged for millions of years. As the old saying goes: "If it's not broken, why fix it?".

Words to look up:

Bore
Protruding
Clinging
Speculate
Evolutionary
Perfection

27

Sea Snails

This group of coral reef animals are well known because when they die, their shells wash up on beaches and are a favourite thing for people to collect. Inside the shell lives a soft bodied creature that is very similar to a garden slug. Like the slug, the sea snails love to eat a vegetarian diet, in this case whatever plants and algae they can find while crawling around the coral reef. Some sea snails are tiny and often go unnoticed, whereas others can grow quite large and are collected and eaten by people, such as the Queen Conch in the Caribbean.

In The Picture: A Tulip Shell with its head buried inside what must be its favourite meal - a delicious looking bunch of algae growing from a nearby rock.

Fun Fact:

One group of sea snail, known as the cone shells, are very venomous. They have a long proboscis with a built-in harpoon which they can use to hunt and capture prey. Even though they are slow moving snails, they are able to catch fast moving fish! Some species of cone snail are so venomous they can even seriously hurt people!

Words to look up:

Vegetarian

Unnoticed

Venomous

Proboscis

Harpoon

29

Sea Slugs

Like the sea snails, sea slugs also eat a vegetarian diet and crawl around the coral reef looking for tasty plants and algae to eat. Some species of sea slug can be very beautiful, with complex ruffles all over their backs that they use to absorb oxygen and breathe. Others can be quite plain and look more like their garden slug relatives. There are a number of other creatures that live on coral reefs and look like sea slugs, some of which are closely related and others that are not. These are featured on the following page.

In The Picture: A Lettuce Sea Slug, so called because it has a collection of ruffles that look just like a salad lettuce that many of us enjoy in our favourite sandwiches.

Fun Fact:

Sea slugs are close relatives of the sea snails, and once had shells of their own. Over evolutionary time however they have lost these shells or they have become incorporated into their bodies so that they can no longer be seen.

Words to look up:

Ruffles

Absorb

Oxygen

Incorporated

31

Sea Slug Relatives

There are a number of other groups of animals that are related to the sea slugs that live on coral reefs. These include the nudibranchs, the shield sea slugs, and the sea hares. They are all soft bodied creatures that browse around the reef looking for their next vegetarian meal, while trying not to get eaten themselves! To help them survive, the sea hares have developed a defence mechanism where they squirt out an inky substance if a predator comes near. This inky substance not only tastes bad but distracts the predator while the sea hare escapes.

In The Picture: A Spotted Sea Hare making its way across a sand flat close to a Bahamian coral reef. This particular creature was very friendly while being photographed and even tried to climb over the camera!

Fun Fact:

Like many coral reef creatures, some of the chemicals produced by the sea hare have medicinal value. Scientists spend a lot of time investigating these substances and then try and use them to cure illnesses. The sea hare for example has been found to produce chemicals that may be able to be used to fight cancer!

Words to look up:

Nudibranch

Browse

Defence

Mechanism

Medicinal

Investigating

33

Worms

Many of the worms found on coral reefs are very different from the ones we find in our back garden vegetable patch. There is a great amount of diversity, from small wriggly ones that swim around in the water and are attracted to light, to large predatory ones that stealthily hunt on the reef for their favourite food. Of the worms, fireworms are a very interesting example, as they have clumps of bristles that protrude from their sides that are toxic and very brittle. If these are touched by other creatures they can snap off in their skin and cause a great deal of pain. A very useful defense!

In The Picture: The head of a Bearded Fire Worm as it folds itself over, and takes a big bite out of, a flexible coral colony (page 12). Fireworms such as this are very active coral predators on reefs all over the world.

Fun Fact:

Of all the worms found on coral reefs, the scariest of all has to be the Giant Eunice, also known as the Bobbitt Worm. This extraordinarily large worm possesses huge, formidable jaws with which it can use to catch fish. It hides silently in its burrow completely hidden, and jumps out seizing hold of it's prey, and then drags it down under the surface. Scary!

Words to look up:

Predatory
Stealthily
Extraordinarily
Formidable
Seizing

35

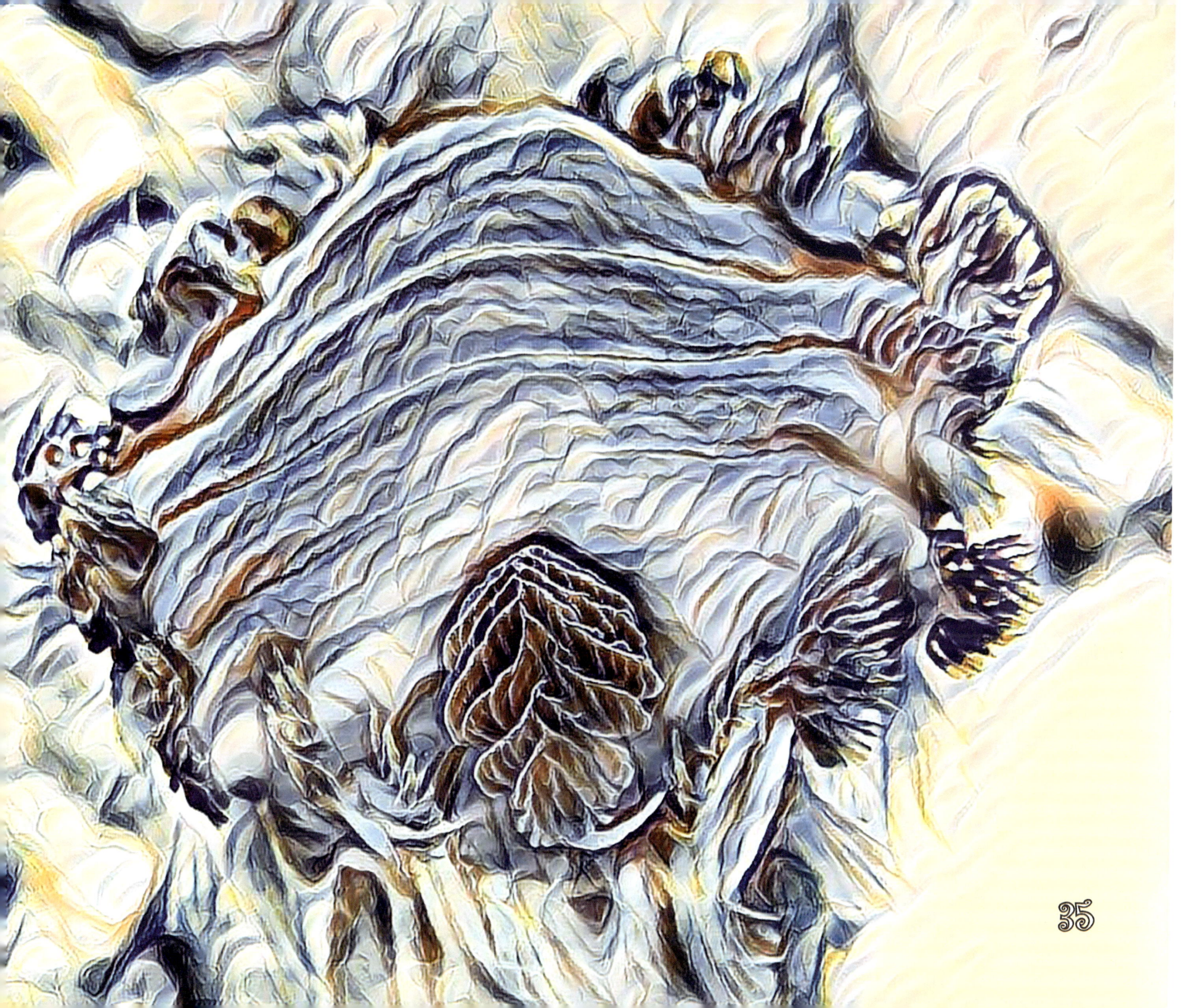

Squid

Squid are very inquisitive and intelligent creatures and are often seen swimming above coral reefs in small groups watching everything that goes on around them. They have the amazing ability to change colour and can camouflage themselves from anything scary by blending in with their background. In a similar way to the sea hares (page 32) they can squirt out ink to help them make an escape from any approaching predators. They can also change their body colour to bright white or dark black to startle or warn off any nearby creatures that are threatening them.

In The Picture: A small Caribbean Reef Squid, no more than a few inches long, takes a long hard look into the camera before squirting out a small cloud of ink and darting off.

Fun Fact:

Squid around the world come in all shapes and sizes. Some are tiny, like the one in the picture, but others are much much bigger indeed! The aptly named Colossal Squid weighs over half a ton and measures up to 10 metres in length!

Words to look up:

Inquisitive
Intelligent
Camouflage
Startle
Aptly
Colossal

37

Octopus

One of the most intelligent creatures who live on a coral reef, octopus are related to squid and can also change their body colour whenever they want, creating amazing patterns and textures that allow them to blend in perfectly with their surroundings. They can also make humps and bumps on the surface of their skin so they look just like the rocks that they are sitting on. If this were not clever enough, they are also able to squeeze themselves through tiny holes in the reef structure and hide away safely from any nasty nearby creatures that may want to eat them!

In The Picture: A Common Octopus making its way up a reef wall during the day. It is the only species of octopus in the Caribbean that comes out during the day as the others are nocturnal.

Fun Fact:

Octopus are incredible and highly intelligent invertebrates, with nine brains, three hearts and blue blood! Scientists who study them have seen that they have advanced problem-solving abilities. In the wild they have even been known to climb onto fishing boats and steal the catch from inside closed boxes!

Words to look up:

Surroundings

Textures

Nocturnal

Invertebrates

Problem-Solving

Abilities

39

Starfish

Starfish are very quiet creatures, that slowly walk around the seabed on hundreds of tiny tube-like feet while they hunt for food. They love nothing more than to catch a tasty crab or clam shell. Their bodies are arranged in a symmetrical pattern, and they have the amazing super power of being able to regenerate parts of their bodies that may get lost during an encounter with one of their enemies. This super power is so amazing that if a starfish gets chopped in half, then each half can grow into a new complete creature! Imagine that!

In The Picture: The Cushion Sea Star is aptly named because it is very fat and puffy-looking just like a comfortable sofa cushion. However, it does have a lot of hard spikes on its surface so maybe not so comfortable after all!

Fun Fact:

Although most starfish live quiet unobtrusive lives, others are far more conspicuous. The Crown Of Thorn Starfish who lives in the Indopacific is one of the largest starfish in the world and can grow up to 35 cm in width and have twenty three arms! They are voracious predators of coral and can cause a lot of damage when in large numbers.

Words to look up:

Symmetrical
Regenerate
Encounter
Unobtrusive
Conspicuous
Voracious

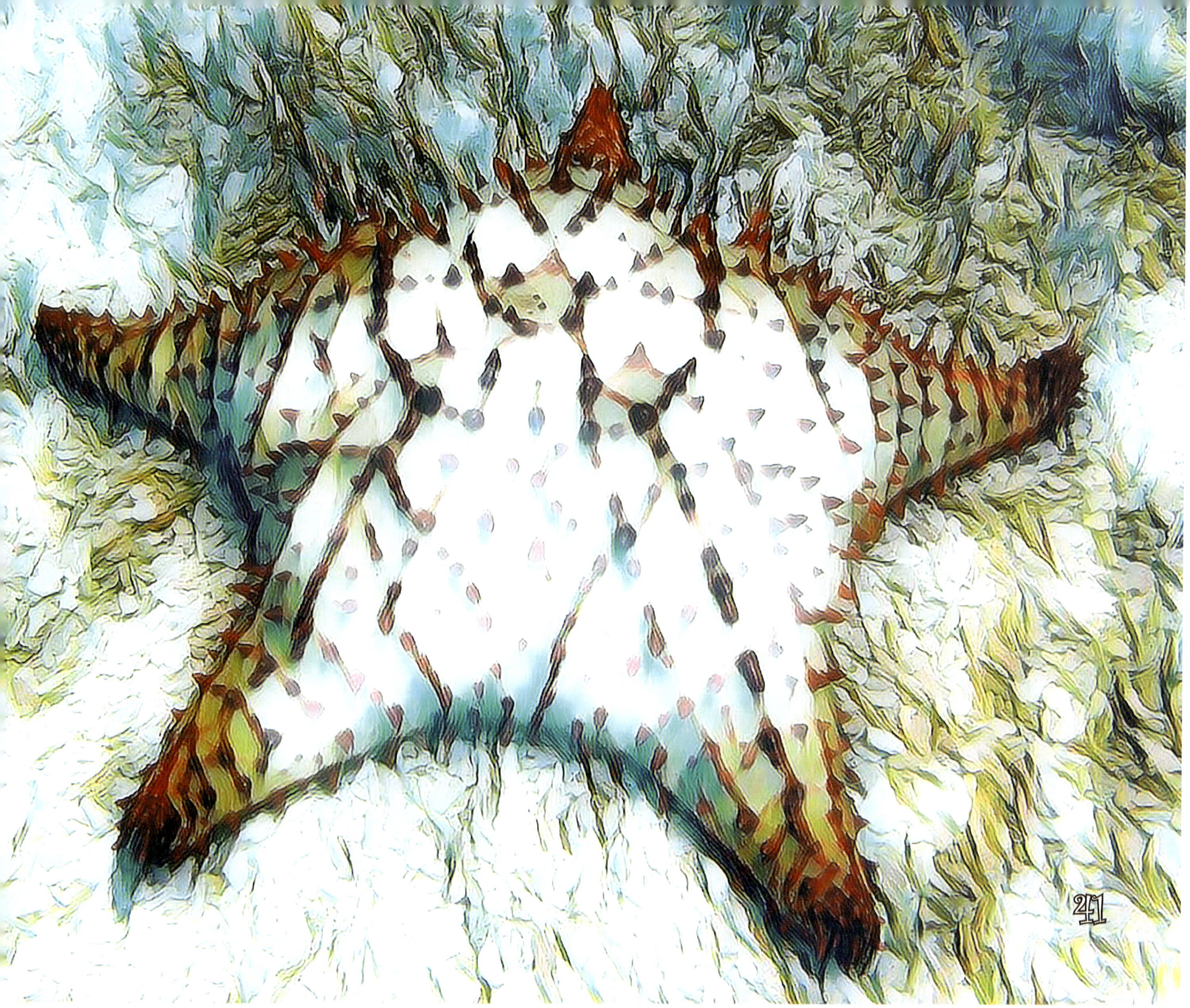

Sea Urchins

Probably one of the most ecologically important group of creatures on a coral reef, the sea urchins have a very big appetite, and consume huge amounts of plants and algae. They eat so much that they are able to clear large reef areas of all vegetation, which is very helpful to corals as it gives them a chance to find a nice clean bit of rock to grow on. Plants and algae grow fast, so without sea urchins corals have a much harder job finding a place to live. Sea urchins are very well defended from predators by sharp and sometimes very long spines, so watch your step! Ouch!

In The Picture: Long-Spined Sea Urchins browsing a coral reef at night. They have extremely sharp spines that can puncture your skin if touched and can be very painful, so as with all underwater life it is better never to touch them!

Fun Fact:

The important role that sea urchins play as a herbivore was recorded during the 1980's by scientists when the Long-Spined Sea Urchin began to disappear from the Caribbean due to an unknown illness. Huge areas of coral reef began to be covered by algae, affecting coral growth. Thankfully their numbers are now recovering.

Words to look up:

Ecologically

Vegetation

Defended

Puncture

Herbivore

43

The Young Explorers Guide to Coral Reef Creatures

Basket Stars

A relative of the starfish and sea urchins, it is quite difficult to see basket stars as creatures sometimes. They rarely walk about, and during the day are curled up in a tight ball and do not move at all. As the sun sets they gradually unfurl their arms, in a similar way to a flower opening. They then use these arms to filter out any food that passes them in the water current and then swiftly eats it. In comparison to the size of their arms their bodies are very small discs, and often cannot been seen unless the creature has stretched open completely.

In The Picture: A Giant Basket Star with its long arms stretched out at night while it feeds. When open like this the Giant Basket Star can be almost half a metre in width, but when curled up by day is not much larger than a tennis ball!

Fun Fact:

Different species of basket star enjoy living in different habitats, from shallow coral reefs to the deep ocean hundreds of metres down. Scientists say that some may live for over 35 years, and the largest species can weigh up to 5 kg. Others choose to live on poisonous sponges to help protect themselves from predators!

Words to look up:

Unfurl
Comparison
Stretched
Poisonous

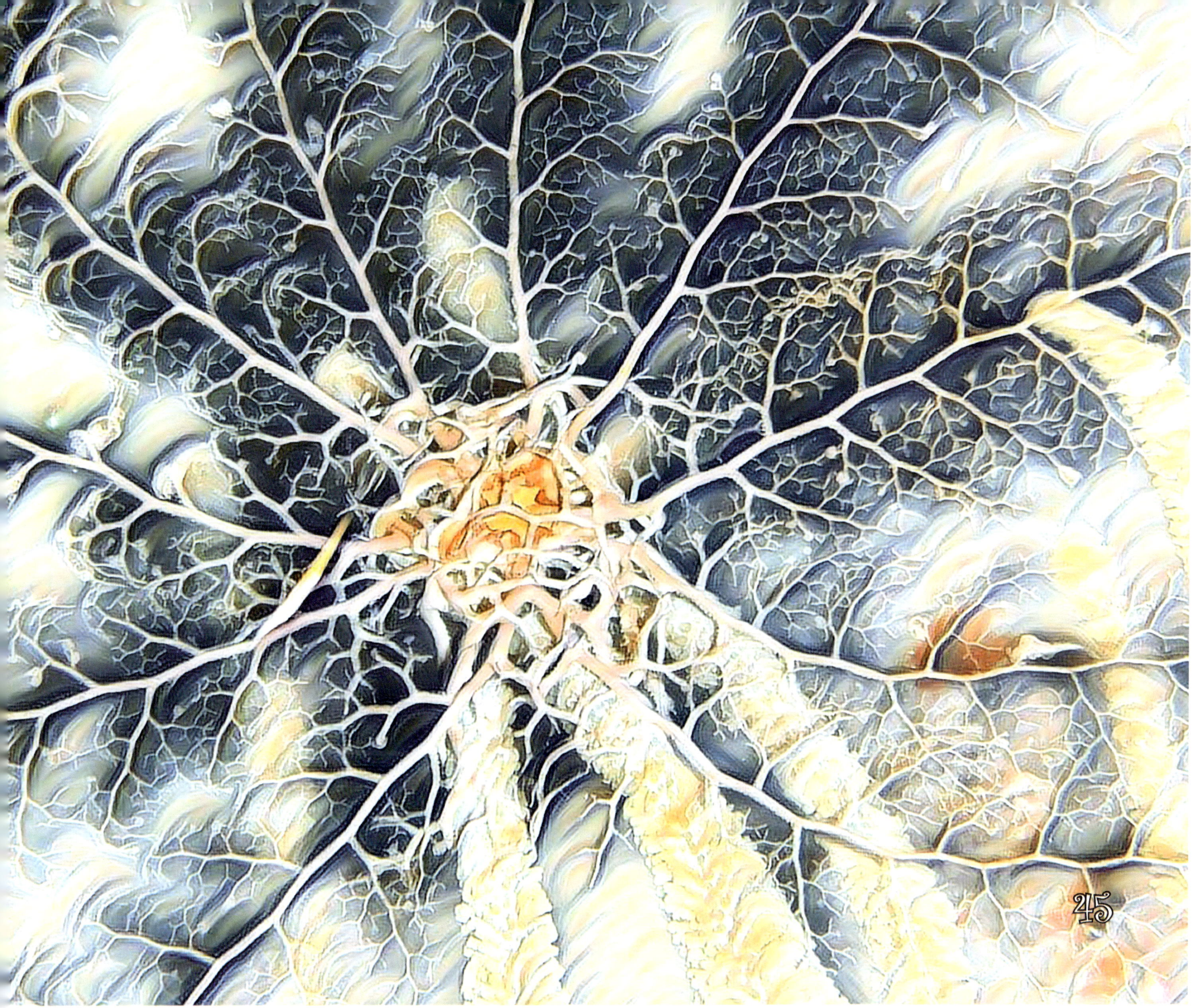

Shrimps

A relative of crabs and lobsters, most shrimps are small creatures that are very hard to see. They sometimes live in the tentacles of sea anemones (page 18) for protection. Other shrimps are a bit larger and walk around the coral reef at night looking for food. They use their tiny claws to lift up small stones and search underneath for tasty treats. Some shrimps use these claws to pick off and eat parasites from fish who visit them specifically for this purpose. The fish enjoy this so much there is often a queue of them waiting to be cleaned!

In The Picture: A Banded Coral Shrimp picking off tasty bits of food from a rock. It has very long antennae which it waves around in the water to sense approaching danger, or feel around with for delicious snacks to eat.

Fun Fact:

Shrimps may be very small but they are very important creatures in ocean food chains. A very closely related type of creature known as krill can form swarms in the water that contain millions of individuals. These swarms are eaten by whales, the largest animals in the ocean. So some of the smallest creatures feed the largest. Amazing!

Words to look up:

Parasites
Specifically
Food Chain
Krill
Swarms

47

Spiny Lobsters

One of the most ornate creatures to live on coral reefs, spiny lobsters are quite beautiful to look at although they are often hard to find because they are most active at night. During the day they like to hang out in small groups inside caves and under crevices where they feel safe and secure. They do not have claws like many other species of lobster, and are instead covered with very sharp spines that help protect them from predators. They also have a pair of thick, spiky antennae that they whip around as a defence, but even so, if an enemy approaches them too closely they can give a very quick flick of their tail and dart off at great speed.

In The Picture: A Spotted Spiny Lobster in a rare picture taken during the day. These spiny lobsters are usually nocturnal and hide deep inside the coral reef structure, only coming out at night to look for food.

Fun Fact:

Although many species of spiny lobster don't wander far from home, others prefer to go on holiday from time to time. The Caribbean Spiny Lobster is one such species. They migrate together during cooler times of the year to find warmer water, marching day and night in long single-file lines until they reach their destination.

Words to look up:

Ornate

Antennae

Whip

Wander

Migrate

49

Slipper Lobsters

These very slow moving types of lobster have no claws, spines or spiky antennae to defend themselves with, instead relying on camouflage and their really thick armour. They hide deep within the reef structure during the day, only coming out at night when they browse the coral reef for food. Like other lobsters, their favourite food items are small worms, sea snails, and general detritus. In the same way as the spiny lobsters, slipper lobsters, although very slow moving, can give a quick flick of their tail to dart away from danger if needed.

In The Picture: The Sculptured Slipper Lobster is one of the most ornately decorated lobster species with a wonderful frill of hairs and spines, and a knobbly mottled-textured body. Beautiful!

Fun Fact:

Slipper lobsters live quite a long time, with some thought by scientists to reach ten years of age. However, compared to other species of lobster this isn't very old at all. The oldest known lobster was named 'George' after being caught in 2008. He was estimated to be 140 years old, and was returned to the sea in 2009. Yay George!

Words to look up:

Armour

Detritus

Frill

Knobbly

Mottled

51

Hermit Crabs

Coral reef hermit crabs, like most hermit crabs around the world, live inside discarded sea snail shells (page 28). Unlike other types of crab, they have a very soft body which they coil inside the sea snail shell, and grip on tightly to it with their tiny back legs. As they grow, the sea snail shell gradually becomes too small for them, so it becomes time to hunt for a new shell. Sometimes when they find one, there are other hermit crabs waiting nearby who are too small for the shell. When the largest crab makes the exchange the others all begin swapping shells with one another, each testing the discarded shells for the best fit. Eventually they all have a new home, and they go off on their way until the next time.

In The Picture: A Caribbean Hermit Crab walking about in an old damaged shell, no doubt on the lookout for a nice new shiny home!

Fun Fact:

Not all hermit crabs live in the water, but they do all still need to live near the sea, returning to it periodically to spawn. The biggest species is called the Robber Crab, which is the largest terrestrial invertebrate in the world. It is almost a metre in length and loves stealing food from beach goers. It is even strong enough to open coconuts!

Words to look up:

Borrow

Exchange

Periodically

Spawn

Terrestrial

53

True Crabs

Crabs come in all shapes and sizes, from tiny little sponge crabs to large armoured king crabs. They all have two claws which they use to forage for food and four pairs of walking legs which they scuttle about on. Some crabs live a very private life, hiding within the reef structure and rarely coming out into the open, whereas others wander around the reef bravely relying on protection from their armoured shells and camouflage. Some even have modified back walking legs that look like paddles, which they use to swim around the reef like true ocean explorers!

In The Picture: A Blue Swimming Crab coming out from its protective hole on a sand flat near a coral reef in the Bahamas. You can see its flattened back legs which it uses for swimming if it needs to get away quickly!

Fun Fact:

Like many of the creatures in this book, crabs can vary greatly in both shape and size. The smallest known crab is called the Pea Crab, which grows no bigger than a pea! Conversely, the largest species is called the Japanese Spider Crab which has a leg span of over three metres making them the biggest crustacean in the world!

Words to look up:

Forage

Scuttle

Modified

Protective

Conversely

Crustacean

55

Coral Reef Conservation

Coral reefs may be huge structures but the coral polyps that build them are very sensitive creatures who are easily damaged. Sadly, over recent decades coral reefs have become under increasing pressure due to over-fishing, global warming and pollution. It has never been more important for humans to act responsibly to help protect these amazing places and the creatures that live within them. We can all do our bit, even if we don't live anywhere near a coral reef, by not wasting electricity and making sure the rubbish in our homes goes in a bin and doesn't end up in the sea. This will help reduce climate change and mean there is less plastic waste in the sea that can damage marine life.

In The Picture: A healthy coral reef in the Caribbean with many types of corals growing and lots of happy fish swimming around. Sadly over recent years sights like this have become less common.

Fun Fact:

Coral reef health was first recorded to be declining sometime during the 1970s when sick corals were found in the Caribbean. At the time it was not known what was causing the sickness, but we now know it is due to human activity and the environmental changes that these activities cause.

Words to look up:

Conservation

Sensitive

Decades

Over-fishing

Global Warming

Pollution

Environmental

57

Index Of Words To Look Up:

Abilities	36	Comparison	42	Environmental	54	Incorporated	30
Absorb	30	Conservation	54	Established	14	Indopacific	18
Algae	4	Conspicuous	38	Evolutionary	26	Inhabitants	14
Antenna	46	Consumed	16	Evolved	8	Inquisitive	34
Aptly	34	Conversely	52	Exchange	50	Intelligent	34
Aquarium	16	Crevices	24	Exoskeleton	22	Internal	10
Armour	48	Crustacean	52	Exposed	8	Intricate	24
Association	18	Decades	54	Fleshy	8	Invertebrates	36
Bore	26	Defended	40	Flexible	12	Investigating	32
Borrow	50	Defense	32	Food Chain	44	Knobbly	48
Browse	32	Detritus	48	Forage	52	Krill	44
Camouflage	34	Diameter	10	Frill	48	Meadows	24
Capture	20	Diversity	8	Global Warming	54	Mechanism	32
Chemicals	16	Diving	10	Gradually	14	Medicinal	32
Clinging	26	Ecologically	40	Habitat	20	Migrate	46
Colonies	2	Elegant	22	Harpoon	28	Minerals	2
Colossal	34	Emergent	14	Herbivore	40	Modified	52
Community	2	Encounter	38	Immune	18	Mottled	48

Index Of Words To Look Up:

Naturalists	8	Pollution	54	Sheltered	16	Threaten	12
Neighboring	4	Polyps	2	Skeleton	4	Toxic	16
Nestled	20	Predator	4	Snorkeling	10	Transparent	6
Nocturnal	36	Prey	6	Solitary	10	Unfurl	42
Nudibranch	32	Problem-Solving	36	Spawn	50	Unnoticed	28
Ocean current	6	Proboscis	28	Species	2	Unobtrusive	38
Ornate	46	Protected	16	Specifically	44	Varieties	8
Over-fishing	54	Protective	52	Speculate	26	Vast	24
Oxygen	30	Protruding	26	Startle	34	Vegetarian	28
Paralyse	6	Puncture	40	Stretched	42	Vegetation	40
Parasites	44	Regenerate	38	Structure	14	Venomous	28
Percent	2	Resemble	12	Substance	12	Voracious	38
Perfection	26	Retracted	4	Surroundings	36	Wander	46
Periodically	50	Rooted	12	Swarms	44	Whip	46
Photosynthesize	4	Ruffles	30	Symmetrical	38		
Plankton	6	Scuttle	52	Tentacles	6		
Poisonous	42	Sea Turtle	24	Terrestrial	50		
Pollinating	24	Sensitive	54	Textures	36		

Look out for book two of The Young Explorers series:

The Young Explorers Guide
To Coral Reef Fishes